Meet Lily

Liliya Oleynik, known to her blog followers as Lily Ardor, is a self-taught artist who resides in Idaho with her husband and son. She was born in Ukraine, and her family immigrated to the United States when she was a toddler. They settled in a little town in northern Alaska where Lily was raised. At an early age, Lily was eager to learn about art! Her journey started with acrylic painting when she was 11 years old, and she moved on to oil painting shortly thereafter. During her teen years, Lily developed an interest in fashion design and attended dressmaking courses.

After she married, Lily and her family moved to Idaho where her husband became an over-the-road truck driver, away from home for three weeks at a time. To keep busy, Lily started a crafting and home improvement hobby, which is where her DIY journey began. In 2017, Lily launched her blog, *lilyardor.com*, where she shares her creations with others. To help and inspire aspiring artists, Lily films her projects and answers questions on her YouTube channel and blog. She likes to work with different art mediums and is always up for a challenge!

You can find Lily on Instagram, Facebook, YouTube, and Pinterest @lilyardor.

Contents

Resin
Creation

Lily Ardor

LEISURE ARTS, INC. • Maumelle, Arkansas

When I think of art, I love to think of the phrase "less is more." #thestruggleisreal

Introduction

When I was first introduced to resin pouring, it was like a new gateway to so many possibilities! Whether you're a beginner or an expert, resin can produce art pieces with amazing depth. I'm not going to lie, the fear of failure had me on freeze mode for quite some time! Resin supplies aren't cheap and winging it didn't seem like an option. That's when I put my research skills into gear and learned all I could before starting my resin art journey! It has been quite the adventure, full of ups and downs that taught me every step of the way. And now, I would love to share it all with you!

This book will help you get started with resin by answering basic questions and helping you master simple techniques to create amazing art! Keep in mind, this book is merely the tip of the iceberg in the world of resin art. There are endless ways to create art with resin!

Most of all, don't forget, **ART HAS NO RULES!** Have fun and embrace who you are as an artist! Ok, let's get started!

Resin 101

In crafting, resin is a two-part substance that consists of a resin liquid and a hardener liquid. Once combined, these liquids harden and become solid. There are many resins to choose from. Some require you to combine equal amounts of resin and hardener liquid, while others have hardener drops that you add to the resin liquid. Some resins are made specifically for art-making, while others are designed for casting and jewelry making.

Types of Resin

Picking the right resin is important as this can make or break your project! The difference between most resins is curing time and clarity. If you're pouring art, it's important to pick a resin that takes longer to cure so you have more time to create your piece. Almost all resins will yellow over time from UV exposure, but some will yellow less than others.

Art resin. Art resin is made specifically for creating artwork. It has a longer working time than other resins. Working time is the amount of time you have to manipulate the resin before it becomes too hard to work with. While most resins only have 15 to 20 minutes of working time, art resin has about 45 minutes of working time. Keep in mind, working time will fluctuate depending on the amount of paint you add to the resin. In most cases, more paint means less working time.

Casting resin. Casting resin is designed for casting projects. It's usually less expensive than art resin and has a shorter working time. That said, you can use other resins, like art resin, for casting projects, too.

Ice resin. Ice resin is a great option for resin jewelry. It gives you crystal-clear results and naturally forms a dome shape, allowing you to fill a bezel or replicate the shapes of stones or gems if desired.

UV resin. This resin is a bit different than the others because it requires a UV lamp or sunlight to cure (the manufacturer's instructions will tell you which). This type of resin has the quickest curing time. Under a lamp, it usually takes seconds or just a few minutes to cure. Under direct sunlight, it takes about 30 minutes to cure.

Mixing Resin

Before using any resin, read the full instructions and safety information provided by the manufacturer.

Most resins work best if they're warm before mixing. If the resin and hardener are cool when mixed, really small bubbles that cannot be popped with heat may form. I like to warm my resin and hardener in a warm water bath for 10 minutes before mixing them.

Pour equal amounts of the resin and the hardener into a plastic measuring cup. (Plastic cups work best for resin. If you use paper cups, the bottoms of the cups will eventually fall out.) It's important to mix equal amounts of resin and hardener for proper curing. If your resin and hardener are not combined properly, your project will not set properly, leaving you with a tacky mess or a flimsy cast.

Use a plastic spoon or a craft stick to gently stir the resin mixture, making sure you scrape the bottom and sides of the cup. Do not whisk, as this will create a ton of bubbles in your resin. Stir the mixture for three minutes. (Some brands only require two minutes of mixing, but I like to do a full three minutes just to be safe.)

Types of resin

Art resin

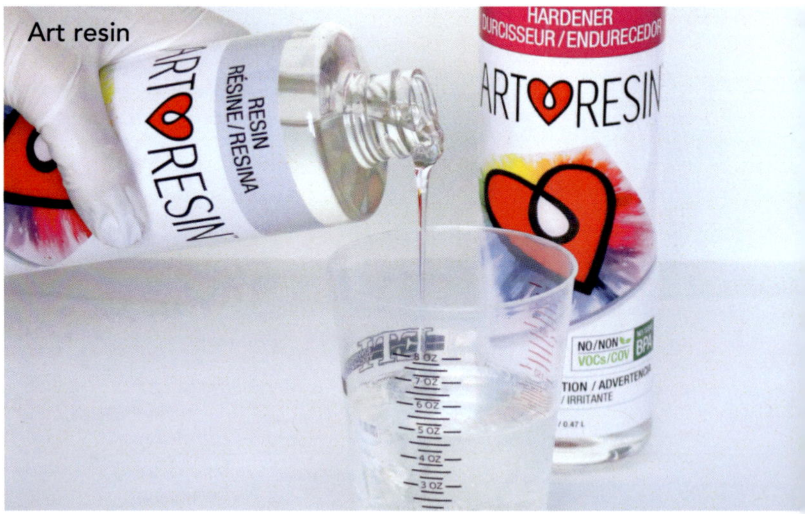

Casting resin

Warm water bath

Resin additives

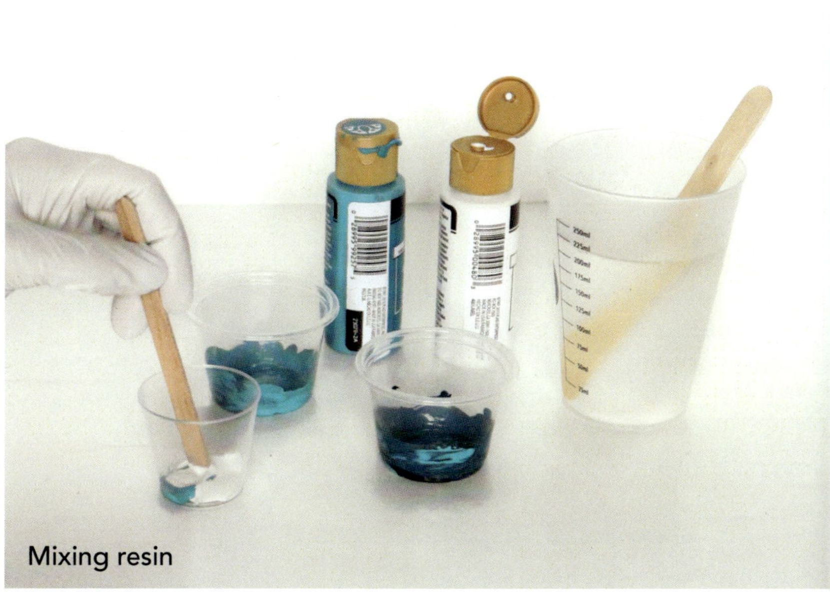
Mixing resin

Measuring Resin

The amount of resin you need for a project depends on what you're making. Every artist has a different way of pouring. Some artists prefer to work with more resin, and some pieces will require more pouring than others.

The number of colors you use also makes a difference because you'll need to mix resin for each color. To minimize waste, I like to mix small amounts of colored resin at a time. You'd be surprised how far a drop of colored resin can go.

You'll need more resin if you plan to cover your work surface with clear resin before pouring. This helps the resin you pour later flow more easily, so you'll use less. I love using this trick when making art!

The chart at the right has some guidelines for the amount of resin I use for different projects. The amounts may vary depending on your project.

Finished Project Size	Amount of Mixed Resin
4" x 4"	1.5 oz
6" x 6"	3 oz
8" x 8"	5 oz
10" x 10"	7 oz
12" x 12"	8 oz
14" x 14"	11 oz
16" x 16"	14 oz

Curing Time

Most resins will be dry to the touch within 24 hours of mixing and fully cured after about 48 hours. Curing time can fluctuate depending on the type of resin and brand you use.

Coloring Resin

There are lots of ways to color resin, including resin tints, liquid pigments, and powders. These are usually very pigmented, meaning you don't have to add much to your resin mixture to get a rich color. But it doesn't end there.

If you have a specific color or effect in mind, you can use acrylic paints, alcohol inks, enamel paints, glitter, and even spray paint with your resin. Different paint brands will react differently with your resin. Some may become darker, and some may cause the resin to harden quicker or even yellow over time. I always like to do a small test batch before mixing a bigger amount of colored resin.

If you plan to combine multiple paint colors to create a new shade, it's important to mix the paint before adding it to your resin. This keeps you from adding too much paint to the resin. If you're trying to get a specific look with metallics, check out page 10 for examples of different metallic additives.

The secret to a successful resin pour is the paint to resin ratio. If too much paint is added, your resin can become clumpy and won't pour well. If using liquid acrylics, be sure to follow the 1 to 10 ratio rule: use 1 part acrylic paint to every 10 parts resin.

It's important to combine the paint with the resin really well to ensure consistent color. Use a craft stick or a plastic spoon and stir to combine the paint with the resin mixture.

Adding Metallics

There's more than one way to add metallics to resin! Alcohol inks, enamel paint, acrylic metallics, spray paint, and powders are just a few of the options you have to choose from. The question is, which one is the best choice for the piece you want to create? Depending on how you apply them, metallic finishes can differ dramatically. Here are a few examples to give you an idea of what each medium looks like.

Spray paint. There are a few ways you can use spray paint with resin. You can spray it on top of poured resin—it's best to do this in small bursts. Or, you can spray the paint into a cup of resin to color it before pouring the resin onto your canvas. The top of the sample photo shows bursts of spray paint added on top of poured resin. The bottom half shows spray paint mixed with the resin before pouring. I used Rust-Oleum® Specialty Metallic spray paint for this piece.

Alcohol inks. Like spray paint, alcohol inks can be added on top of poured resin (as shown in the top of the sample photo) or mixed with the resin before pouring (as shown in the bottom). I used Pinata alcohol inks in Brass and Gold for this piece.

Enamel paint. Enamel paints act very similarly to alcohol inks, and it's often hard to tell the difference between the two. The top of the sample photo shows enamel paint added on top of the resin after pouring, while the bottom shows enamel paint mixed with the resin before pouring. I used Testors® enamel paint in Gold – Metallic and Silver – Metallic for this piece.

Powders and acrylic paint. Metallic powders and acrylic paint are very similar. They work best when added to resin before pouring, but you'll notice their color changes dramatically when mixed with the resin. The resin brings out the color's

Metallic additives

Spray paint

Alcohol inks

Enamel paint

Powders and acrylic paint

orange hues and reduces the metallic effect. The top of the sample photo shows metallic acrylic paint added to the resin before pouring while the bottom shows metallic powder added to the resin before pouring. I used Golden® acrylic paint in Iridescent Gold Deep (Fine) and Pearl Ex Powdered Pigments™ in Aztec Gold for this piece.

Adding Texture

Resin will adhere to so many things! You can add pebbles, rocks, crystals, sand, seashells, or pretty much any solid, dry item to a resin piece. There are a few ways to do this. You can add items to your resin mixture before pouring. You can also hot glue items onto your project surface and then pour resin over them (this works well with bigger rocks or pebbles). You can also add items to resin that's already been poured. Any items added to poured resin will settle into the resin and adhere.

Applying a layer of 3D paste to your project surface before pouring the resin is also a great option for adding texture. Just make sure your 3D paste is completely dry before pouring resin over it.

Creating Lacing

Adding silicone oil to your resin creates beautiful lacing and cells in your art. Silicone acts as a repellent, so lacing will appear in any resin mixed with silicone oil and also any resin poured on top of it.

Lacing can also be created by using resin with different densities. When you mix resin with paint to add color, you change the resin's density and weight. Because of this, once the resin is poured, some colors will settle quicker than others, creating a lacing effect.

Working with different densities is a great method, but it can take a few tries to master. Your results will vary depending on the paint brand and colors you use and how you apply air to your piece. My heat gun has very light airflow and works perfectly to push out cells in resin. You can also blow air through a straw to target specific areas.

I've also noticed lacing appear wherever white resin is thinned out, either using a heat tool or the wax paper technique on page 15.

Silicone can give your artwork amazing lacing and cells, but it can yellow your art over time.

Popping Bubbles

Every time you stir your resin, especially when adding paint, bubbles will build up in the mixture. To fix this, I like to hold a heat gun on the bubbles for a few seconds before pouring my resin. See page 12 for more info about using heat tools.

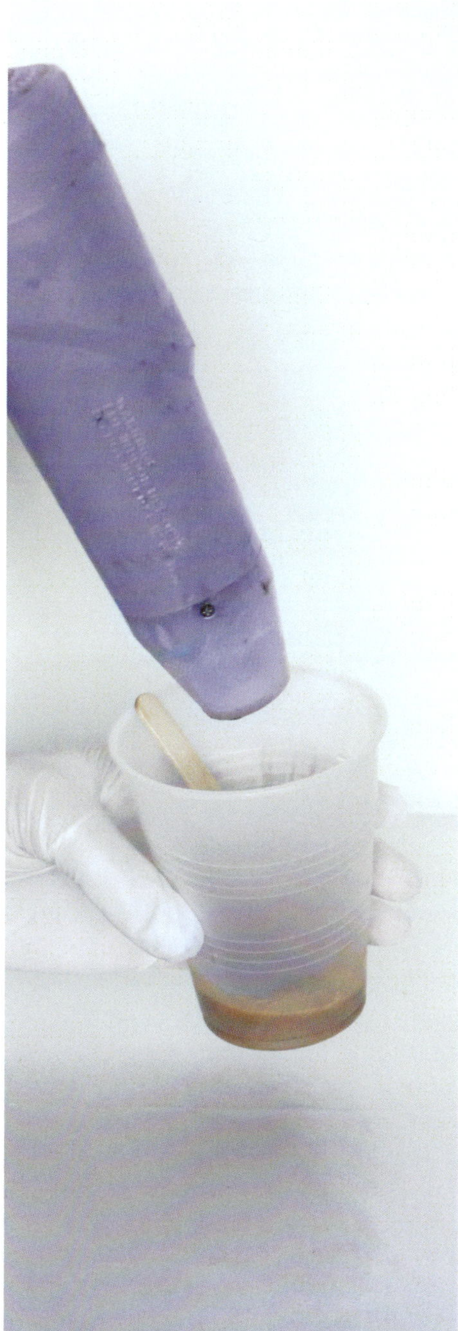

Popping bubbles

> **Tip**
>
> If you want to break items like beads into smaller pieces before adding them to your resin, place them between some paper towels and hit them a few times with a hammer. I use this method to crush beads all the time! The mess is minimal, and it works well to break up the pieces the way I want for my finished piece.

Crushed turquoise

Tools & Materials

To work with resin, you'll need some basic tools and materials.

- Plastic mixing cups
- Plastic measuring cups
- Plastic spoons or craft sticks
- Toothpicks
- Straws
- Tape
- Gloves
- Lots of napkins
- Respirator mask
- Heat gun or blowtorch
- Blow-dryer
- Level
- Wax paper or cardboard (for surface protection)
- Plastic cover or cardboard box (to protect your art while curing)

Using Heat Tools

Once your resin is poured and starts to settle, you'll notice bubbles rising to the top. A heat gun or blowtorch will help you remove these bubbles. Every artist has their preference for heat tools, and depending on the type of art you're making, one might work better than another. I use a heat gun most often because it blows a small amount of air. This gives me great control when blending colors and popping bubbles. If you don't want movement in your colors, I'd recommend a blowtorch.

Please use caution when working with heat tools, as they can burn the resin or present a fire hazard if not used properly. Always have a fire extinguisher on hand. Resin will burn if you hold a heat tool in one spot for too long, hold it too close, or go over the same area too many times. Burnt resin will become rubbery and stringy. To pop bubbles, hold your heat tool 2 to 3 inches from the surface of the resin and move it continuously. It should only take a few seconds to pop bubbles.

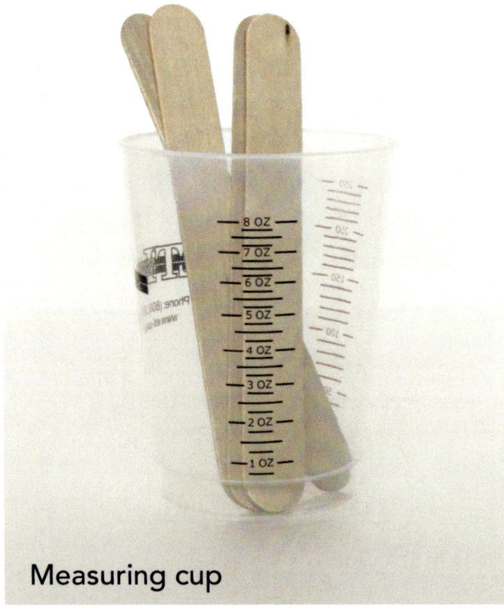

Measuring cup

Attach cups to canvas

A Note About Blow-Dryers

A blow-dryer is great for giving your poured resin movement and blending colors. Use the low setting on your blow-dryer and hold It on your poured resin from a distance. Blow-dryers do not work to pop bubbles—even on a low setting, the air comes out so strongly that the resin will move around before any bubbles can be popped.

Resin Pouring Basics

There are no rules when it comes to resin pouring surfaces. Some of the most popular are canvas, medium-density fiberboard (MDF), wood, plywood, wood canvas, or glass. That said, solid surfaces work best. If you're not sure about which surface to use, test some options before attempting the full project.

Preparation

Preparing your pouring surface is one of the most important steps for a successful pour. To keep your project from being stuck to your work surface, it's best to elevate your pouring surface. I do this by hot-gluing small plastic cups to the back of my pouring surface. This allows the resin to pour off the edges nicely. Once the resin cures, I remove the cups.

Sometimes, you might not want the resin to pour off the sides of your project. In this case, use tape to create a barrier around the sides of your pouring surface to keep the resin in place. Once the resin cures, remove the tape.

A level surface is a must when pouring resin. If your pouring surface is not perfectly level, the resin will flow toward the lowest area. While your work surface may be level, your pouring surface may not be, especially after you attach cups to the back. So always use a level to check that your pouring surface is level and make adjustments as needed.

Priming wood or canvas surfaces is not required. However, there are upsides to priming and every artist has their preference!

In addition to preparing your pouring surface, it's also important to prepare your workspace. Because resin has a limited working time, it's so important to have everything at arm's reach! When working on a project, I like to keep a ton of napkins, extra gloves, craft sticks, straws, toothpicks, and cups to my left. On my right, I have all my pebbles, paints, and a sheet of cardboard or wax paper for trash. I don't like to throw anything out right away because I sometimes find those materials come in handy for finishing touches. So I keep them close by until I'm completely finished with the project.

Working on Canvas

I usually don't prime canvases because white canvases sold in stores already come with a coat of gesso on them. (Gesso is an art primer that binds to surfaces really well.) The only time I apply additional gesso is when I want an extra smooth surface. I use a brush to apply a nice thick coat of gesso to the canvas. Once it's dry, I lightly sand it down for a smooth surface.

If you're working on a big canvas, it may sag in the middle during pouring. Prevent this by propping the middle of your canvas up with a piece of cardboard. Or you can try something sturdier like MDF or wood.

Working on Wood

I like to apply gesso to wood only when I need a white surface to work on. I usually apply one coat of gesso and let it dry completely before sanding it down a bit. When I want the look of raw wood in my project, I leave the wood unprimed.

Pouring Multiple Layers

You can pour multiple layers of resin in one art piece. Lots of artists use this technique to create amazing designs! Here's the best way to do it: Pour your first layer, wait 3 to 12 hours, then pour the next layer. Repeat as desired. Waiting several hours between pours instead of letting the resin fully set before adding the next layer will give you the best adhesion between layers.

Resin Casting & Jewelry Making Basics

Resin casting is a fun way to make jewelry or even home décor pieces. You can use casting resin when working with wood or to fill molds.

Silicone molds work best with resin. The resin doesn't adhere to the silicone, so it can be removed from the mold easily once cured. There are ways to make your own molds if you have a specific shape in mind. Check out the ice cube earrings on page 44 to learn more!

You can add almost any dry, solid object to a resin cast—pebbles, rocks, beads, glitter, dried flowers. I've even seen M&M's® cast in resin! If you're unsure about adding something, do a test before using it in a project. Check out the flower coasters on page 56 for a tutorial on how to dry flowers for use in resin projects.

Once your resin cast is fully cured, you can paint over it. It's best to prime the resin surface before painting to ensure the best results. I like spray primer because it creates a clean, even coat. Once your primer is completely dry, use acrylic paint to put the desired finishing touches on your project.

Once resin is cured, it is safe to drill through it. This is great if you're making jewelry and need to add jewelryhardware (also known as findings).

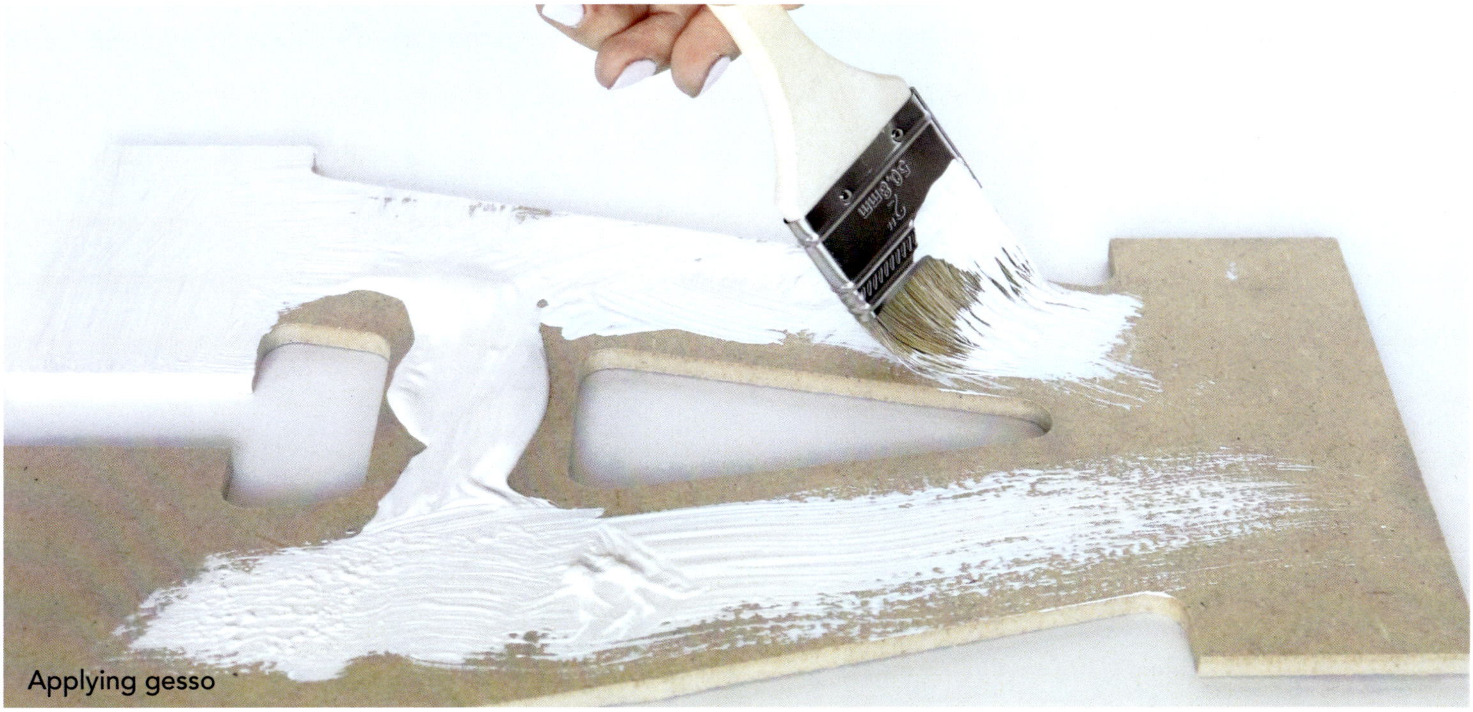

Applying gesso

Seascape Collage

This canvas collage uses three different techniques to create ocean-inspired art. Before starting a project, I like to sketch out a quick draft in pencil to help envision what I plan to make. It helps me determine how many colors and what shades I need to mix.

Supplies

- Art resin
- Acrylic paint in Titanium White (FolkArt®), Navajo Turquoise (FolkArt®), Black (Ceramcoat®), Lite Mocha (Apple Barrel®), and Mustard Yellow (Craft Smart®)
- One 12"-diameter round canvas
- One 10"-diameter round canvas
- One 8"-diameter round canvas
- Seashells
- Pebbles
- Sand
- Strainer
- Comb
- Measuring cup
- Mixing cups
- Craft sticks
- Wax paper
- Duct tape
- Heat tool

Tip

Always leave some of your resin mixture uncolored for touchups or in case you need to mix more of a specific color.

Wax Paper Technique

1. **Mix the resin.** Place the 12" canvas on a flat, level surface. Then, mix the resin and separate it into cups. Add a different paint color to each cup, making sure you keep some clear resin as well. If you plan on mixing multiple paint colors to create a new shade, always premix the paint in a separate cup before adding it to the resin. I mixed 8 oz of resin total and used 6 colors: 3 shades of blue, 2 shades of sand, and white.

2. **Pour the resin.** Pour each color onto the canvas. Start with the darkest blue at one end of the canvas and work inward with the next two shades of blue. Leave a 1½" space in the center of the canvas, then pour the dark sand color followed by the light sand color, taking the light sand all the way to the other end of the canvas.

3. **Fill the center.** Pour clear resin onto the space you left in the center of the canvas. Then, pour white resin on top of it. This will help keep the white resin clean as you move it with wax paper. If you want the white to blend with the other colors, skip pouring the clear resin. Be sure to add plenty of white to the center of the canvas—it thins out quickly once you start moving it with the wax paper.

1

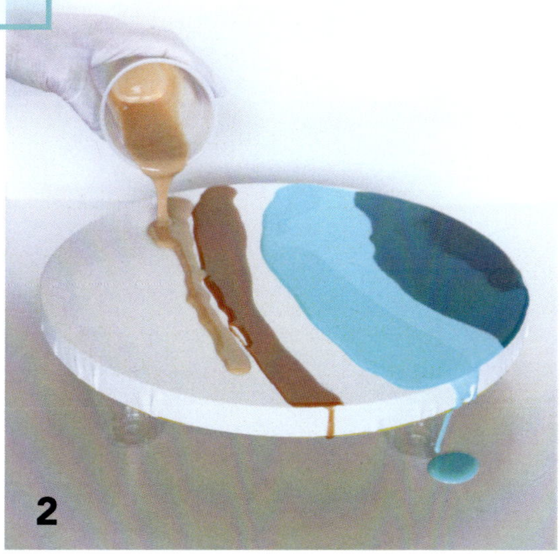

2

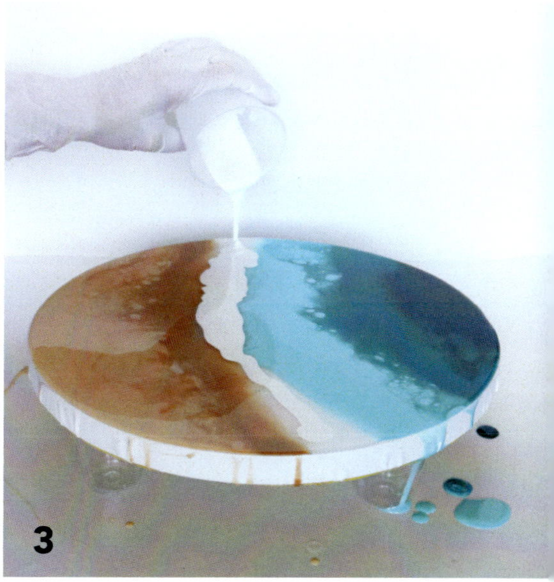

3

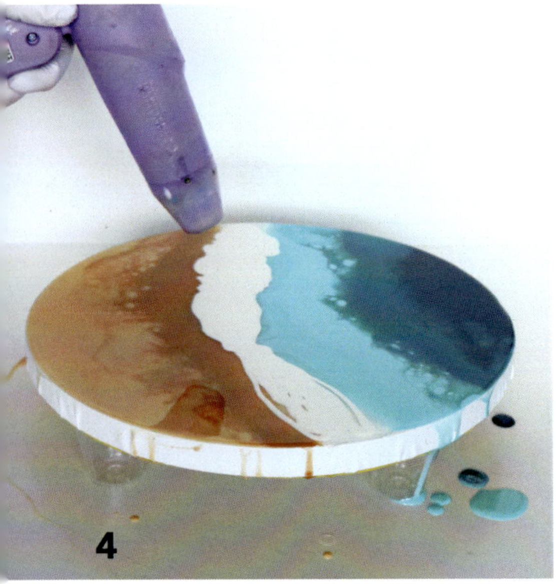

4

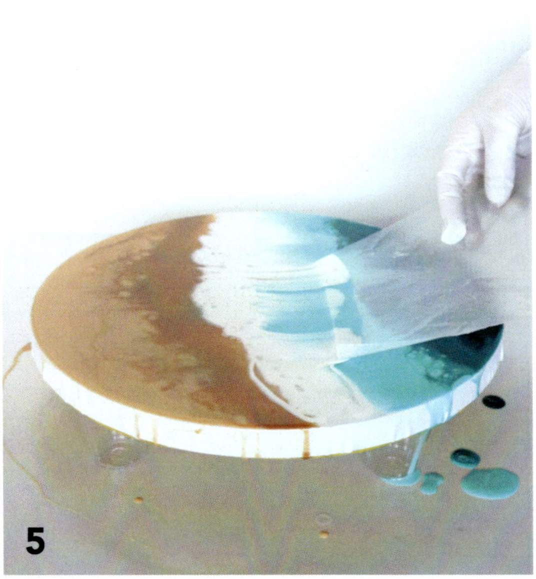

5

6

4. **Pop any bubbles.** Use a heat tool to pop any bubbles in your resin. Hold the heat tool about 2" to 3" away from the resin and move it over the surface continuously. (See page 12 for more info on using heat tools.) Once the resin is warm, it will become runny and easy to work with.

5. **Blend the white.** Cut a piece of wax paper and gently place one end on the white resin. Don't apply any pressure—the wax paper will adhere to the resin on its own. Gently pull the wax paper toward the blue resin to move a layer of white resin over the blue. You can pull the wax paper all the way off the end of the canvas or pull it a few inches and then lift to create wisps. Thinner pieces of wax paper work best for creating wisps. When you've finished with the wax paper, use your heat tool to blend the colors a bit more. Heat guns are gentle, but very hot, which is great for controlled blending.

6. **Finish.** Add some pebbles, shells, and sand to finish off the piece. I also blew some of the white resin onto the sand-colored resin to enhance the seashore look.

Strainer Technique

1. **Prepare the canvas.** Cover the sides of the 8" canvas with duct tape, forming a barrier to keep the resin from running off the canvas during pouring. While you can always elect to let the resin pour off the sides of your canvas, I find this particular pattern tends to disappear if the resin is allowed to move.

1

Tip

Cover your finished project with a plastic container or a cardboard box to protect the resin as it cures.

2. **Mix the resin.** Mix the resin and separate it into cups. Add a different paint color to each cup, keeping some clear resin as well. I mixed 5 oz of resin total and used 4 colors: 3 shades of blue and white. To create a distinct pattern, you'll need at least 2 colors for this project, a dark color and white or a pale color. For example, blue and pale yellow or purple and pale pink.

3. **Pour the resin.** Place the strainer in the center of your canvas. Pour the resin into the strainer, alternating between dark and light colors. If you have different shades of the same color, make sure you pour white or another color with different intensity between each shade. Every time you add a color, the resin beneath it will be pushed outward. Don't force the resin out of the strainer—this technique only requires you to pour and watch the magic happen.

4. **Finish pouring.** Continue pouring resin until it starts coming out of the holes on the sides of the strainer. Once the resin starts settling, it will spread out, so you don't need to worry about covering the whole canvas. I kept pouring until about three-fourths of my canvas was covered.

2

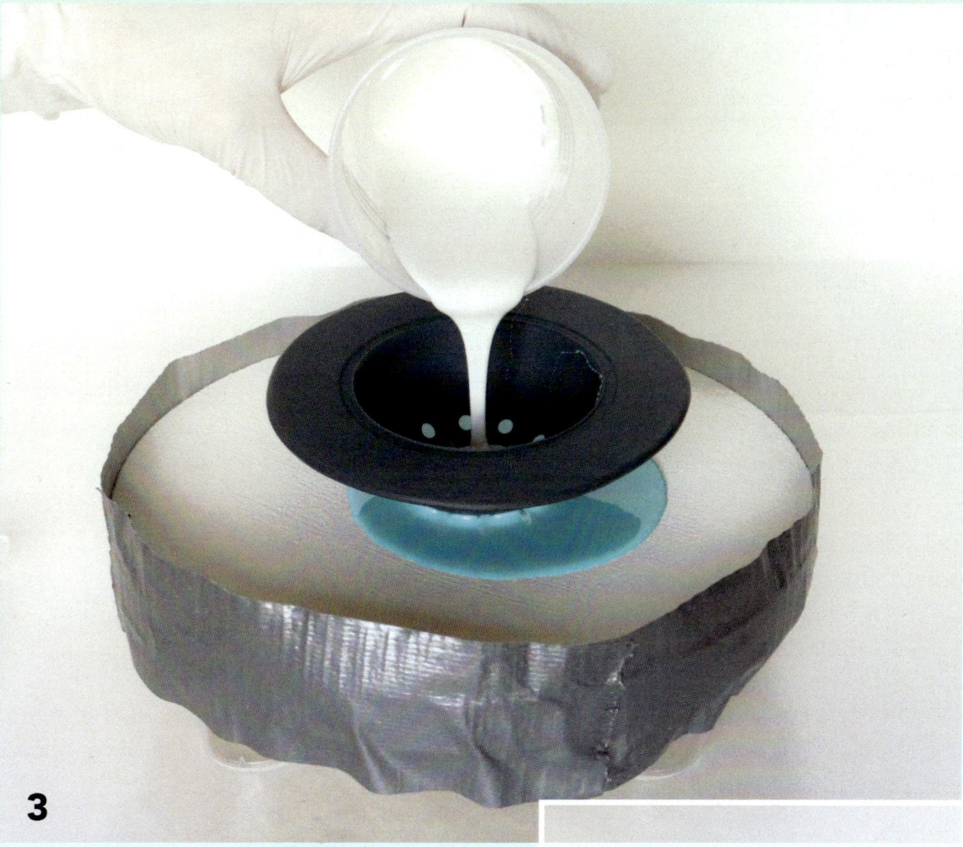

3

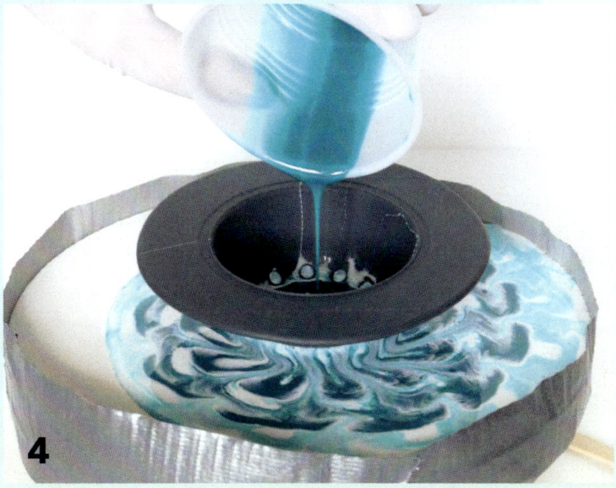

4

Tip

To avoid lots of bubbles in your art, pop them inside the cups before pouring by holding a heat tool over them for a few seconds. Heating the resin also makes it runnier, which helps it flow through the strainer easily.

5. **Finish.** Remove your strainer by quickly lifting it off the resin. Finish the piece by pouring resin around the edges of the canvas to cover any empty spaces. You can use clear or colored resin for this. Add finishing touches like pebbles, shells, or sand around the edges. I dipped a toothpick in white resin and used it to trace lightly around my pebbles to enhance the seashore effect.

Tip

Resin tends to move away from objects placed on top of it. Depending on the effect you're going for, you may want to avoid adding pebbles near the center of your design.

5

Hair Comb Technique

1. **Mix the resin.** Mix the resin and separate it into cups. Add a different paint color to each cup, keeping some clear resin as well. I mixed 7 oz of resin total and used 4 colors: 3 shades of blue and white.

2. **Add the pebbles.** Add some pebbles to the edge of the 10" canvas. I mixed the pebbles with some uncolored resin and poured the mixture onto the canvas. You can also add pebbles on top of the poured resin, keeping in mind that resin tends to move away from objects placed on top of it. This can create a really cool effect depending on the look you're going for.

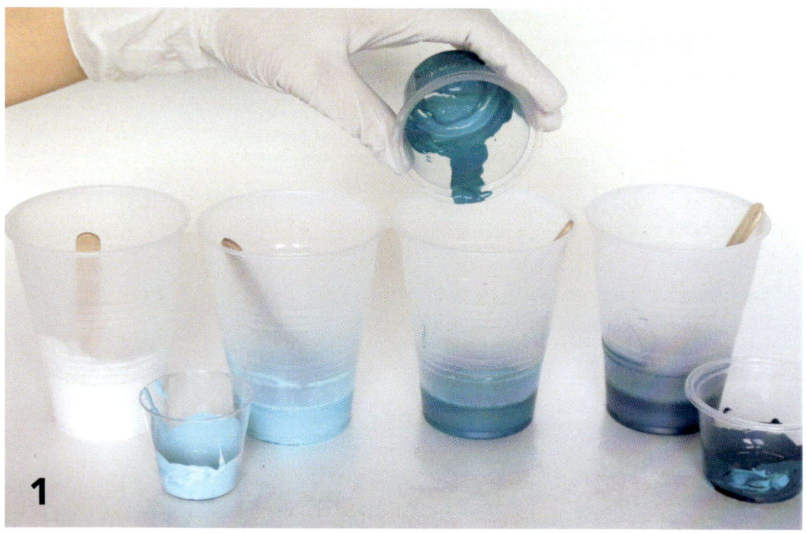

1

2

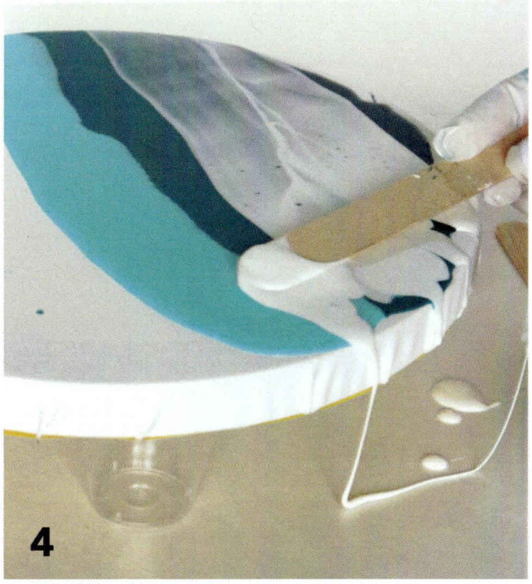

3. **Pour the resin.** Starting at the end of the canvas opposite the pebbles, pour the colored resin (except the white). Start with the darkest color and add the lighter colors as you work toward the pebbles. Leave a 3" space between the lightest color and the pebbles. Use a heat tool to pop any bubbles in the resin.

4. **Add the white.** Dip a craft stick into the white resin and lightly spread it over the colored resin. This works best if you do it in one swipe. It's ok if you can't, just don't go over the same area twice to keep the colors from mixing. Don't apply too much pressure—you want the white resin to sit on top of the blue.

5. **Create the pattern.** Gently drag a comb through the white resin, starting at one end of the canvas and moving to the other end. You'll end up pushing resin off the edge of the canvas with the comb, and that's ok. If you want, move the comb up and down a bit as you drag it across the canvas to create wavy lines.

6. **Finish.** Add clear or colored resin to the empty spaces on the canvas (I used clear). You can also pour colored resin over the pebbles to make them pop. Remove any bubbles with a heat tool.

Plum Pebble Clock

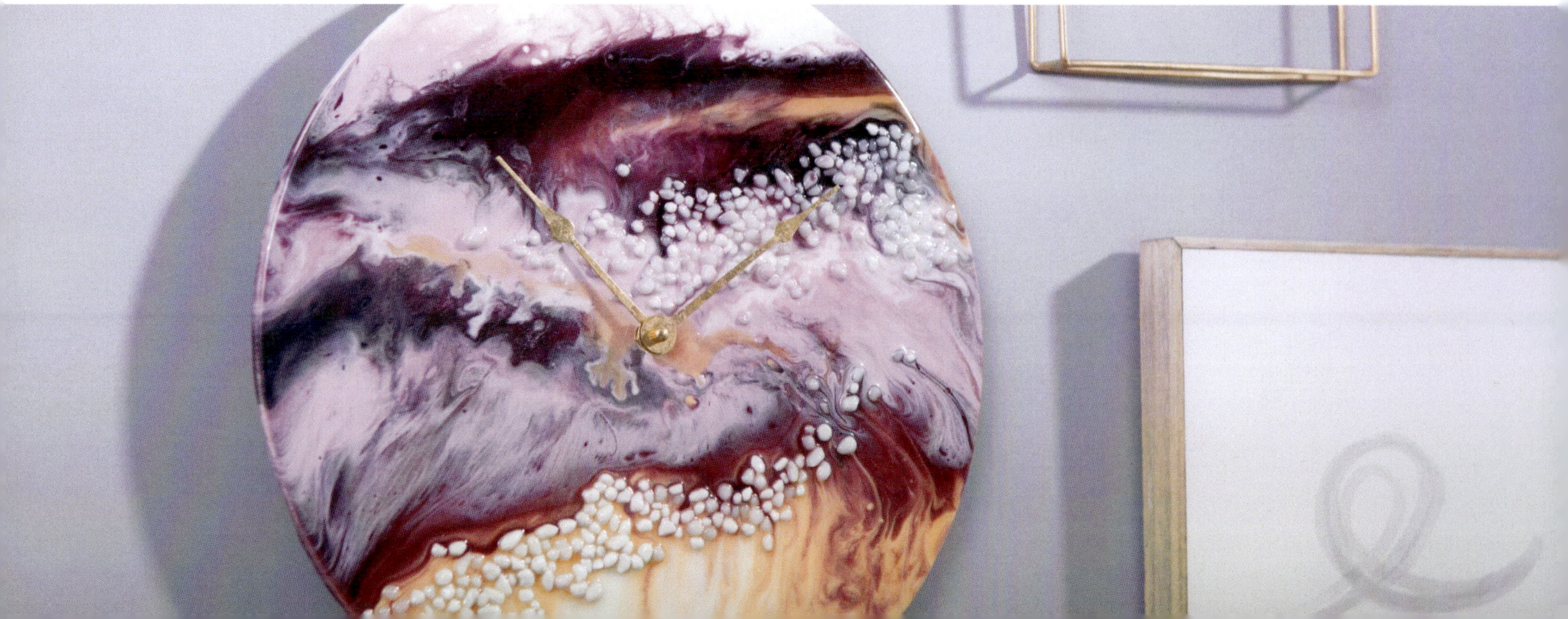

This project will teach you how to build depth and texture in a design, all while keeping the resin from running off the edges of your surface. In the end, you'll have a mesmerizing piece of art you'll be proud to display!

Supplies

- Art resin
- Acrylic paint in Dark Plum (Anita's™), Cinnamon (FolkArt®), Titanium White (FolkArt®), and Black (Ceramcoat®)
- 12½"-diameter round wood board
- White pebbles
- Measuring cup
- Mixing cups
- Craft sticks
- Tape
- Clock movement
- Drill
- Heat tool

1. **Prepare the wood.** Add tape to the back of the wood, placing it in a ring around the edge. This extra tape on the back will help you remove any resin that builds up as the piece cures. Use tape to cover the sides of the wood, forming a barrier so the resin won't spill over the edges during pouring.

2. **Mix the resin.** Mix the resin and separate it into cups. Add a different paint color to each cup, keeping some clear resin as well. I mixed 8 oz of resin total and used 6 colors: lavender, pale orange, dark orange, white, and dark plum/purple. I also mixed a tiny bit of black to add depth to some areas.

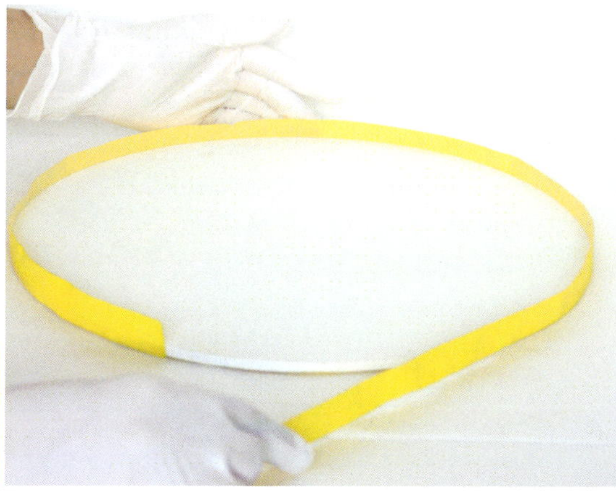

1

2

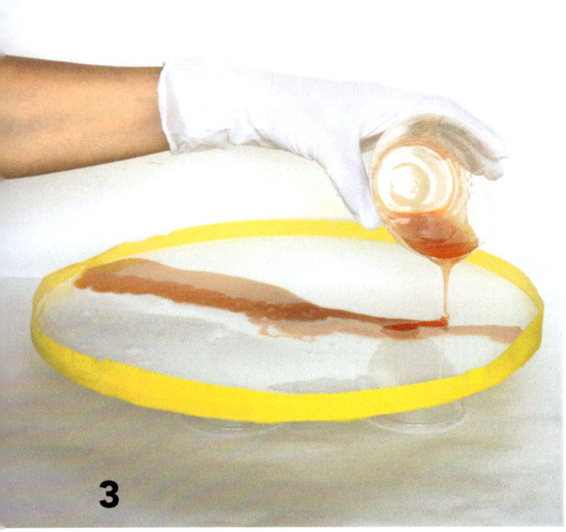
3

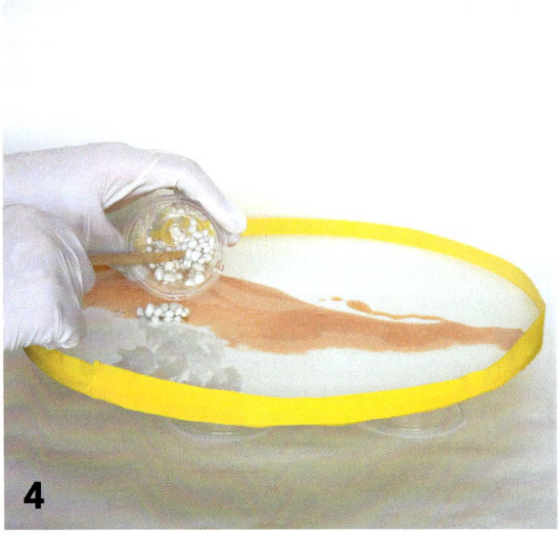
4

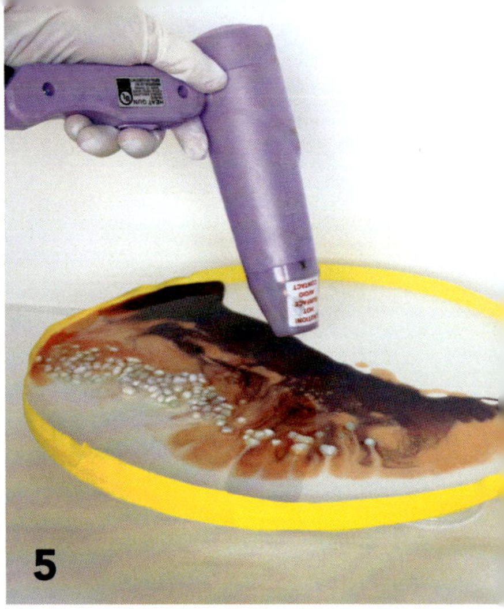
5

3. **Pour the resin.** Pour white resin over half of the wood surface. Then pour the pale orange followed by the dark orange over the middle.

4. **Add the pebbles.** If you'd like, add pebbles to the area where the white and orange resin meet. You could also use crystals, sand, seashells, or any other dry, solid object. (Resin hates moisture!)

5. **Add the plum.** Pour a thin strip of plum resin along the other edge of the orange resin. Use a heat tool to gently blow the plum resin onto the orange. This will also push the resin over the pebbles, creating beautiful texture and depth. I also added a tiny bit of black resin where I thought the plum color needed more depth. A drop of black goes a long way!

6. **Finish pouring.** Repeat Steps 3–5 on the other side of the wood, using lavender instead of orange. I added lavender, then a line of pebbles, then several thin lines of color. Then, I used my heat gun to blend the colors a bit.

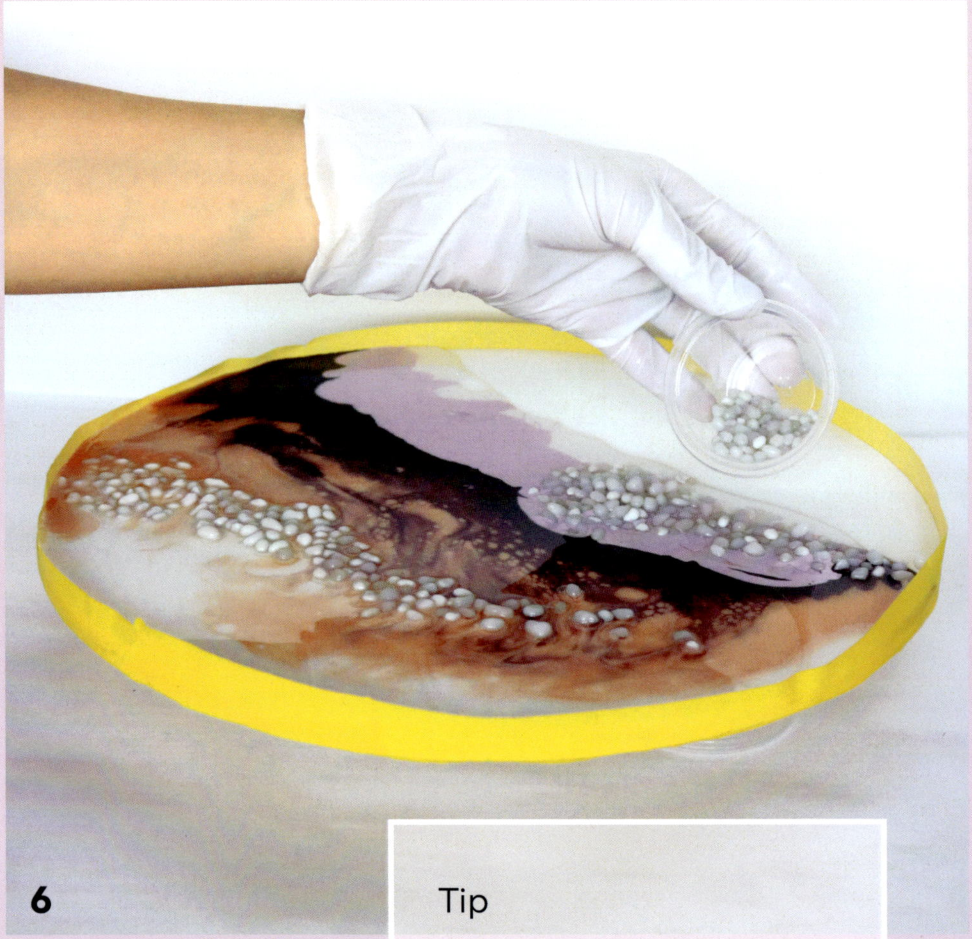
6

Tip

Have fun experimenting with the colors you use for the pebbles and the resin. White pebbles look great with dark resin blown over them and vice versa.

7. **Finish.** Once you've finished pouring and blending the resin, remove the tape from the sides of the wood, and let any extra resin spill over the edges. This will shift your design slightly. You can keep the tape on until the resin cures if you'd like. Let the resin set for 24 hours, then remove the tape from the back of the wood. This should remove any resin drips that accumulated on the back of the piece while the resin set. If you want to turn this piece into a clock, wait until the resin Is fully cured, then drill a hole in the center and install the clock movement.

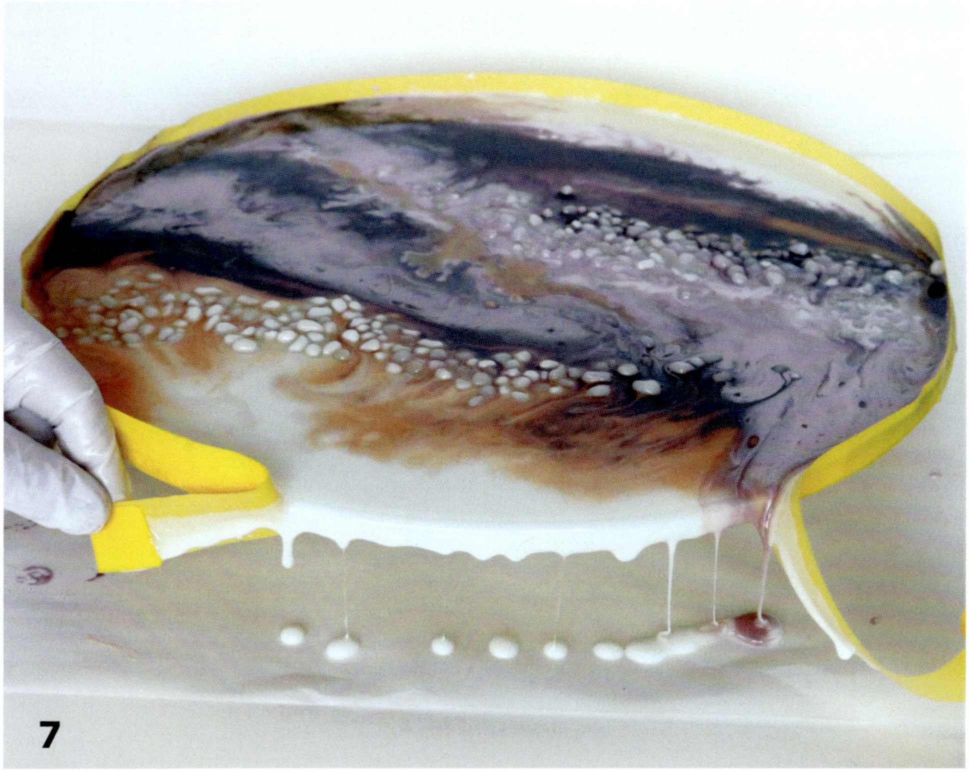

7

Color Burst Coasters

Alcohol inks take resin to a whole new level!! If you want to make bold, colorful art, give them a try. These coasters are a thrill to make. You never know what pattern the alcohol inks will produce, so it feels like a surprise every time you pull a finished piece out of the mold.

Supplies

- Casting resin
- Alcohol ink in Iris (Copic® ink refill B79), Petroleum Blue (Copic® ink refill BG07), Forest Green (Copic® ink refill G17), Special Black (Copic® ink refill 110), Mustard (Brea Reese™), Magenta (Brea Reese™), Brown (Brea Reese™), Baja Blue (Pinata), and White (Pinata)
- Silicone mold
- Craft stick
- Measuring cup
- Mixing cups
- Heat tool

1. **Pour the resin.** Wipe down your silicone mold to ensure the surface is as clean as possible. Mix the resin and let it sit for 3 to 4 minutes. Use a heat tool to pop any bubbles that rise to the surface, then pour the resin into the mold. I wanted my coasters to be about ¼" thick, so I poured a ¼" layer of resin.

1

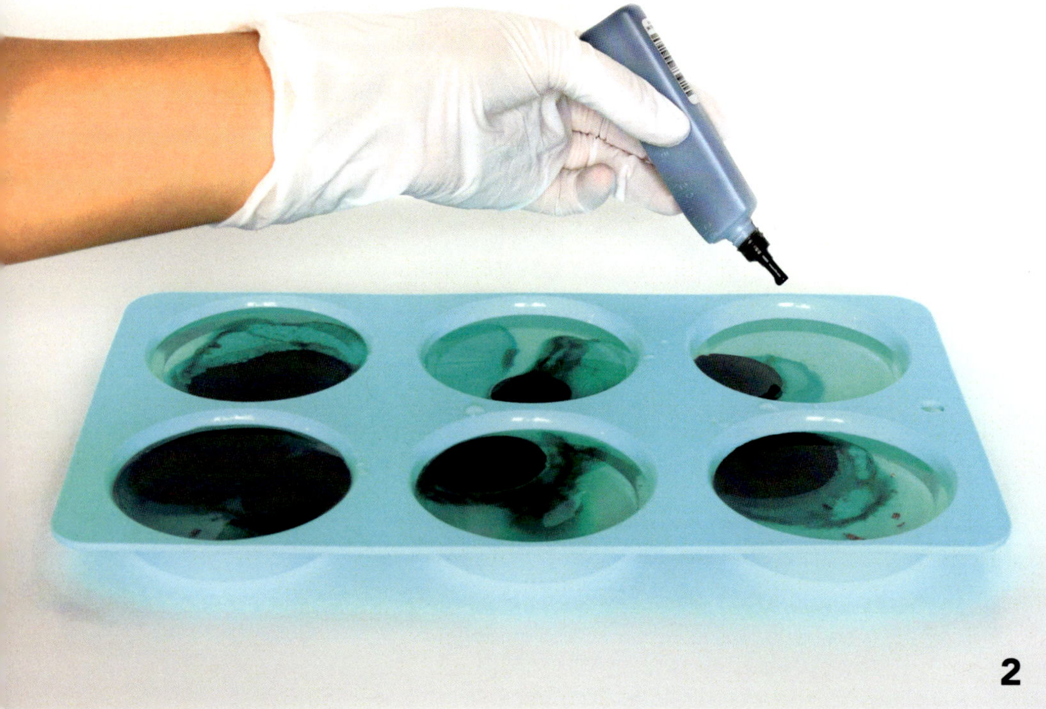

2

2. **Add the alcohol ink.** Add drops of alcohol ink to the poured resin. I combined the purples and yellow for some coasters and the blues, green, brown, and black for the others. Don't add too much ink or the resin will take much longer to cure and may not set properly. The spaces in my mold were about 3" in diameter, and I added 7 to 15 drops of ink to each. The less ink you add to the resin, the more translucent your coasters will be.

3. **Finish.** To give your coasters a burst effect, add drops of white alcohol ink to each one. You'll need white ink to create this effect—it can't be done with another color. I added about half as many white drops as colored drops for each coaster (about 4 to 8). Let the resin cure for 24 hours before removing the coasters from the mold.

3

Seascape Initial

Lacing is an effect many artists like to create in their artwork. This project will teach you how to use silicone oil to create defined and beautiful lacing in your resin art. While I chose to use an initial for my pouring surface, you can use any shape you'd like!

Supplies

- Art resin
- Silicone oil
- Acrylic paint in Cinnamon (FolkArt®), Navajo Turquoise (FolkArt®), Persian Red (Master's Touch®), Titanium White (Master's Touch®), and Black (Ceramcoat®)
- 13"-tall MDF initial
- Pebbles
- Craft sticks
- Measuring cup
- Mixing cups
- Straw (optional)
- Hot glue gun and glue sticks
- Heat tool

1. **Add the pebbles.** Hot glue some pebbles to your initial to add texture. I had some lava rocks around the yard that came in really handy for this piece.

2. **Mix the resin.** Mix the resin and separate it into cups. Add a different paint color to each cup, keeping some clear resin as well. I mixed 8 oz of resin total and used 6 colors: turquoise, pink, 2 shades of tan, black, and white. Measure 1 oz of white resin and add 5 to 8 drops of silicone oil to it. You can experiment by adding silicone oil to more colors.

1

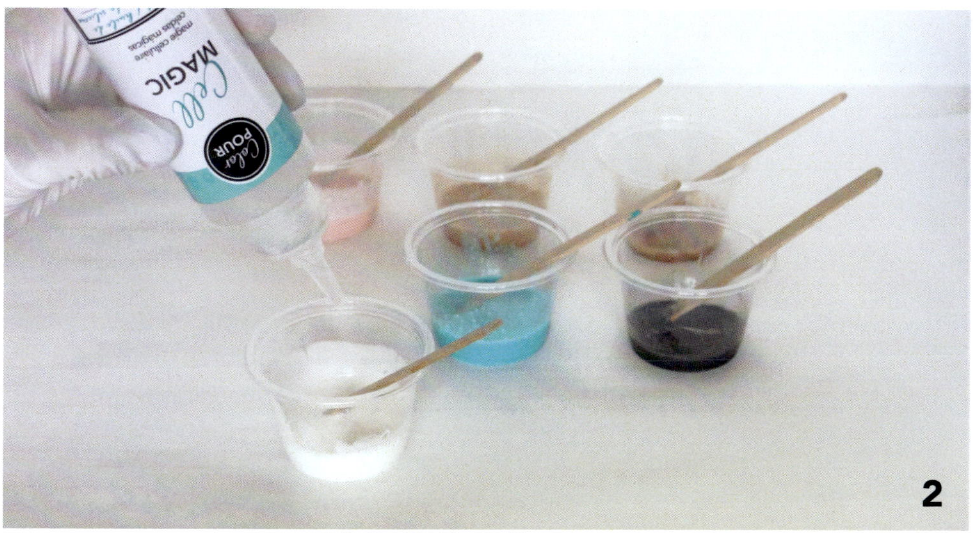

2

3. **Pour the resin.** Pour black resin around the pebbles and use a heat tool to pop any bubbles. Heating the resin also helps fill all the spaces between the pebbles. Pour the colored resin (except the white), leaving spaces anywhere you want to add the white resin. Start with the blue resin along one side of the initial. Then add the pink to the other side. Add the two tan colors near the bottom.

4. **Create the lacing.** Pour the white resin mixed with the silicone oil wherever you want cells to appear. Use your heat tool to gently move the white resin around. Lacing will start to appear as it mixes with the colored resin. You can also use a straw, a fan, or condensed air to move the resin around. If you don't see enough lacing, add a few more drops of silicone oil to the white resin.

3

4

Tip

Test your silicone oil resin in a small area first to make sure you've added enough silicone oil to create the amount of lacing you'd like.

Marbled Canvases

Metallics can add the perfect touch to any art piece! Resin works well as a clear finish for artwork like an acrylic or watercolor painting. But adding metallics to the resin finish will take your art to a whole new level.

Supplies

- Art resin
- Alcohol ink in Iris (Copic® ink refill B79), Forest Green (Copic® ink refill G17), Special Black (Copic® ink refill 110), Warm Gray (Copic® ink refill W5), Green Gray (Copic® ink refill BG93), Pale Cherry Pink (Copic® ink refill R11), and Brass (Pinata)
- Two 5" x 7" waterproof panels (I used ones from Brea Reese™)
- Measuring cup
- Mixing cups
- Craft stick
- Straw (optional)
- Blow-dryer

1. **Add alcohol ink.** Drip one color of alcohol ink onto your canvas and move it around with a blow-dryer until it is dry. Repeat with as many colors as you'd like to create the desired effect on each canvas. I used the grays and pink for one canvas and the purple, green, and black for the other canvas. Let the ink dry completely before moving to the next step.

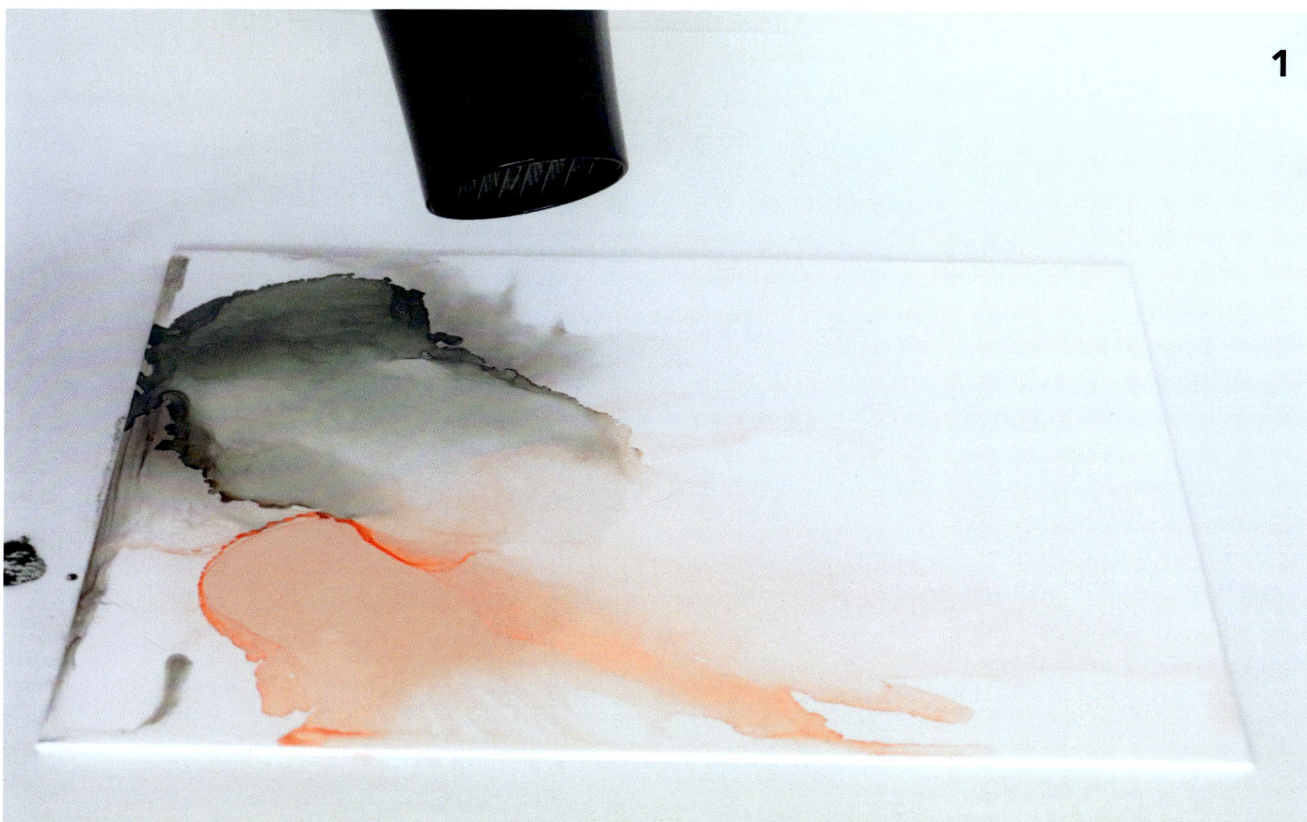
1

2

2. **Pour the resin.** Mix the resin and pour it on top of your canvases. Once the resin is poured, add a few drops of metallic alcohol ink on top. You can also experiment with pouring tinted resin on top of your canvases to create depth in the layers.

3. **Finish.** Use a heat tool or blow-dryer to gently move the resin and metallic ink around. I also like to blow air through a straw if I want to focus on specific areas. When added after pouring, alcohol ink floats on top of resin, which means you can create some amazing wispy effects when you move it around with your heat tool. If desired, add another layer of clear resin to seal the metallic ink.

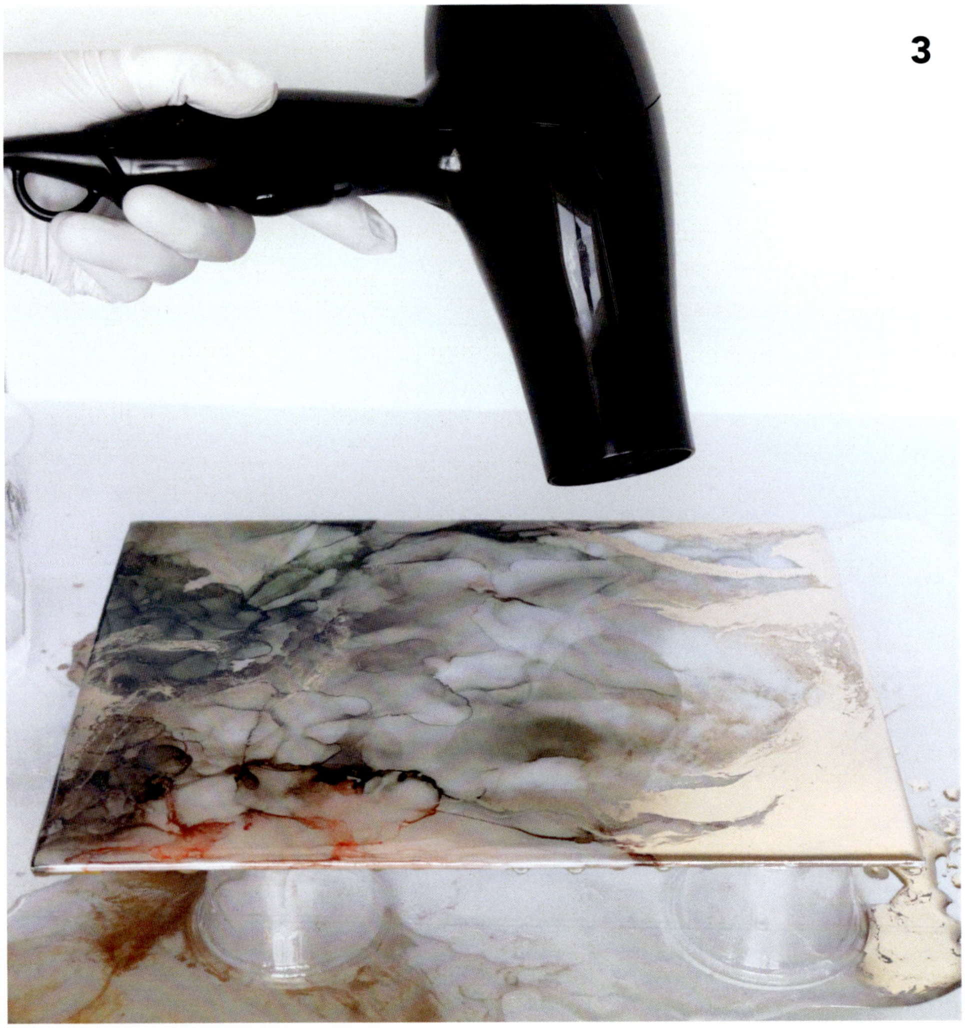

3

Wood Slice Tray

Wood home décor pieces are timeless. And now, resin and wood have become a popular combination. I used craft wood slices for this tray, but you can use any dry material to create the same effect.

Supplies

- Casting resin
- Acrylic paint in Titanium White (Master's Touch®)
- 12" square wood tray
- Craft wood slices
- Measuring cup
- Mixing cups
- Craft sticks
- Paintbrush
- Screwdriver
- Hammer
- Hot glue gun and glue sticks

1. **Prepare the wood slices.** You can keep your wood slices whole or use a hammer and screwdriver to split them into smaller pieces.

2. **Secure the wood slices.** Arrange the wood pieces in the tray and hot glue them in place. This will keep them from shifting around when you pour the resin.

3. **Seal the wood.** When using wood and resin, it's important to seal the wood with a thin layer of resin before pouring. Sealing the wood keeps any wood dust from mixing with the poured resin and also reduces bubbles. Mix a small amount of resin and use a paintbrush to seal the tray and wood slice pieces.

1

2

3

4. **Pour the resin.** Mix more resin and color it using the acrylic paint. Pour the colored resin, filling the spaces between the wood pieces, but not covering them. Use a paper towel to wipe away any resin that ends up on top of the wood pieces. You can also use clear resin and cover the wood pieces completely.

5. **Finish.** Some of your wood pieces will be thicker than others. To create a level surface for the bottom of your tray, wait for your colored resin to cure, then mix and pour a layer of clear resin on top.

4

5

Crystal Geode

Geodes are great inspiration for resin art—they have a pretty pattern of rings, sparkly crystals, and unbelievable colors! They sparkle and shine and almost seem magical. This project shows you how to make the perfect mold for a resin geode, create a stunning crystal center, and replicate the mesmerizing burst effect.

Supplies

- Art resin
- Acrylic paint in Evergreen (Americana®) and Purple (Pentart)
- Silicone
- Clear plastic sheet (I used a table protector)
- Clear beads
- Gold leaf
- Gold leaf adhesive
- Gold leaf sealer
- Measuring cup
- Mixing cups
- Craft sticks
- Toothpick
- Paintbrush
- Wire cutters
- Hot glue gun and glue sticks
- Heat tool

1. **Make the mold.** Sketch the shape of your geode on a piece of paper and place it under the plastic sheet to use as a guide. Trace the geode shape with the silicone, making a silicone wall that's at least ½" tall.

2. **Add the beads.** Hot glue some clear beads in the center of your mold. Don't worry about the hot glue being visible—it will be covered by the resin later. Glue some large beads in a circle and fill the center with smaller ones. Use plenty of hot glue so the beads don't shift around later when you're using your heat gun. Keep in mind, you can always add more beads once your resin has cured.

Tip

If the colored resin doesn't move toward the center of the mold after you've added the clear resin, you can use a toothpick to help. Gently dip the toothpick into the colored resin and drag it toward the center. Repeat as needed to create the desired effect. This technique works well with light colors.

1

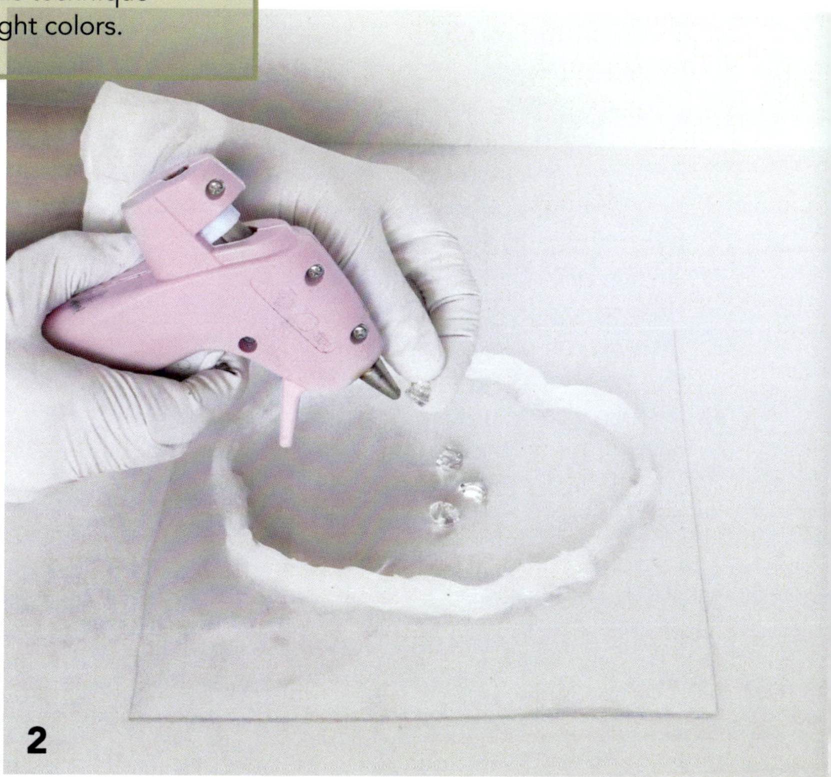

2

3. **Pour the colored resin.** Mix the resin and color some of it, keeping the rest clear. My mold was 4" in diameter, and I used 2 oz of resin. This technique works best with dark colors, which produce a really cool burst effect. if you want to use a light color, you can create the burst effect with a toothpick, as I did for the purple geode. Apply a thin line of colored resin along the inner edge of the mold.

4. **Pour the clear resin.** Add a ring of clear resin inside the colored resin and use your heat gun to warm it up a bit. You will see the clear resin start to pull the colored resin toward the center of the mold. If you're using a light color, use a toothpick to draw the colored resin through the clear resin to create the burst effect.

5. **Finish.** Fill any remaining space in the center of the mold with clear resin. If this impacts the color burst, use your heat tool to warm the resin again and move the color where you want it. Pop any bubbles with the heat tool. If desired, add a few drops of colored resin to the beads in the center—a little goes a long way. Once the resin has cured, remove it from the mold and trim away any rough edges. Apply gold leaf to the edges and seal.

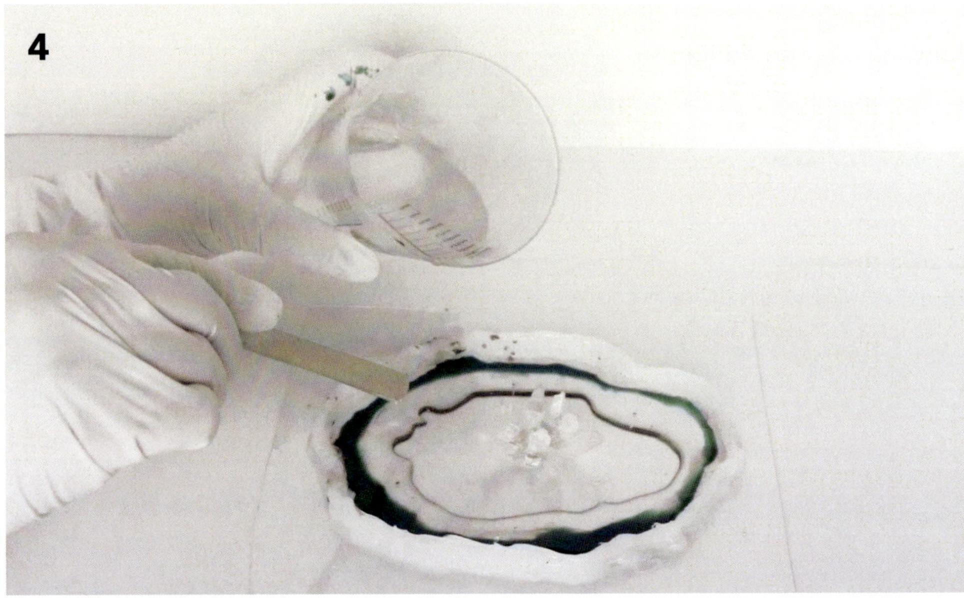

Ice Cube Earrings

Casting resin is perfect for jewelry making. You can make your creations even more unique by using mold putty to make custom molds. Mold putty is easy to use, and it works well with resin, so you can get as creative as you'd like with your jewelry pieces.

Supplies

- Ice resin
- Mold putty
- Spray finish
- 2 mini wood blocks
- Dried mini flowers
- 2 screw eye pins
- 2 kidney wire earring hooks
- Measuring cup
- Mixing cups
- Craft stick
- Sandpaper
- Tweezers
- Wire
- Wire cutters
- Heat tool

1. **Make the molds.** I sanded my wood blocks to remove as much of the wood grain as possible so the pattern would not be imprinted on the putty. Mix the mold putty and wrap it around the wooden blocks to make mini cube molds. Leave one side of the blocks uncovered so they can be removed from the molds once they're cured. Wait about 20 minutes for the putty to set. You'll know it's cured when you can push your fingernail into it without leaving a mark. Remove the wooden blocks from the molds.

2. **Add the flowers.** Add some mini flowers to each mold. I added one or two long stems to each mold and made sure they were held in place by the walls of the mold so they wouldn't break loose when the resin was poured.

Using Mold Putty

Just like resin, mold putty is made of two substances that harden and become like hard silicone when combined. Once combined, it takes mold putty about 20 minutes to set. Once the putty has set, you can easily remove any objects you used to shape your mold and begin casting.

1

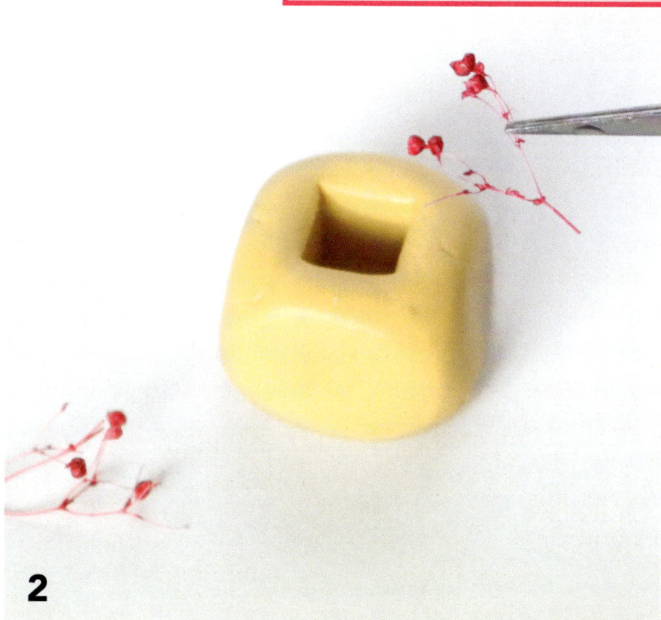

2

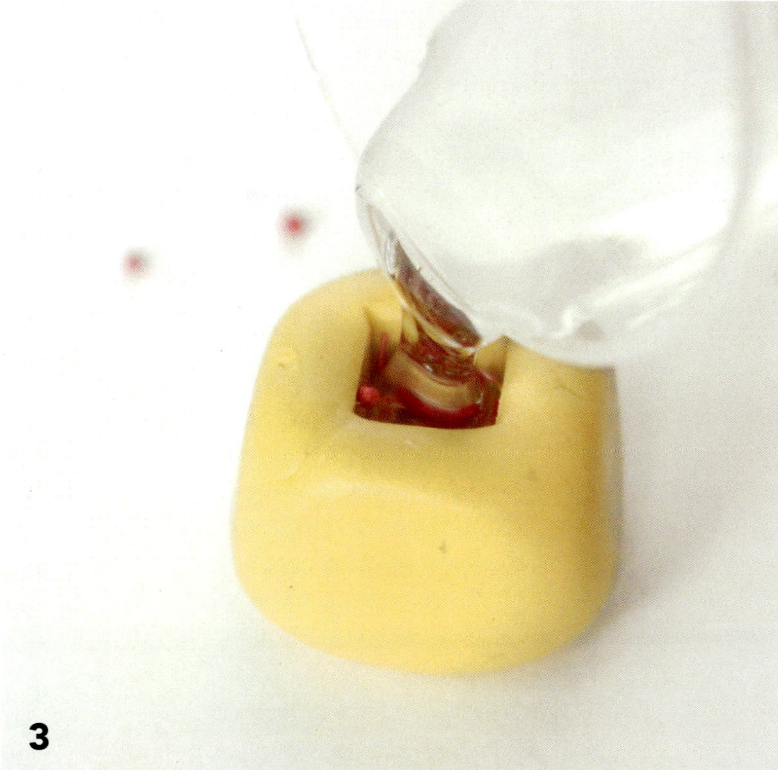

3

4

3. **Pour the resin.** Mix the resin and set it aside for a few minutes. Use a heat tool to pop any bubbles that float to the top. Fill each mold about three-quarters full with resin. Then add a few more flowers.

4. **Finish.** Feed a piece of wire through each screw eye pin. Use the wire to position a screw eye pin over the opening of each mold. Fill the molds the rest of the way with a few more drops of resin, making sure the resin covers the bottoms of the screw eye pins. Let the resin cure for 24 hours before removing it from the molds. Use wire cutters to trim away any sharp edges. Seal the resin with a spray finish. Attach an earring hook to each screw eye pin.

Seashell Pendant Earrings

There are endless ways to make jewelry with resin, and sometimes recycled materials make the cutest molds. Something as simple as a drinking straw can be used to make unique pendants for earrings or a necklace.

Supplies

- UV resin (I used Lisa Pavelka Magic-Glos™)
- 2 screw eye pins
- 2 kidney wire earring hooks
- Sand
- Crushed turquoise
- Seashells
- Tape
- Toothpick
- Clear plastic straw
- Wood block
- Craft knife or scissors

1. **Cut the straw.** Cut a 1½"-long piece off each end of the straw and discard the middle. It's important to use the ends of the straw only because they have clean cuts and will adhere perfectly to the tape in Step 3.

2. **Position the tape.** Place a piece of tape sticky side up on a level surface (I used a wood block) and secure the ends with more tape. Use tape with good adhesive to keep the resin from seeping between it and the straws.

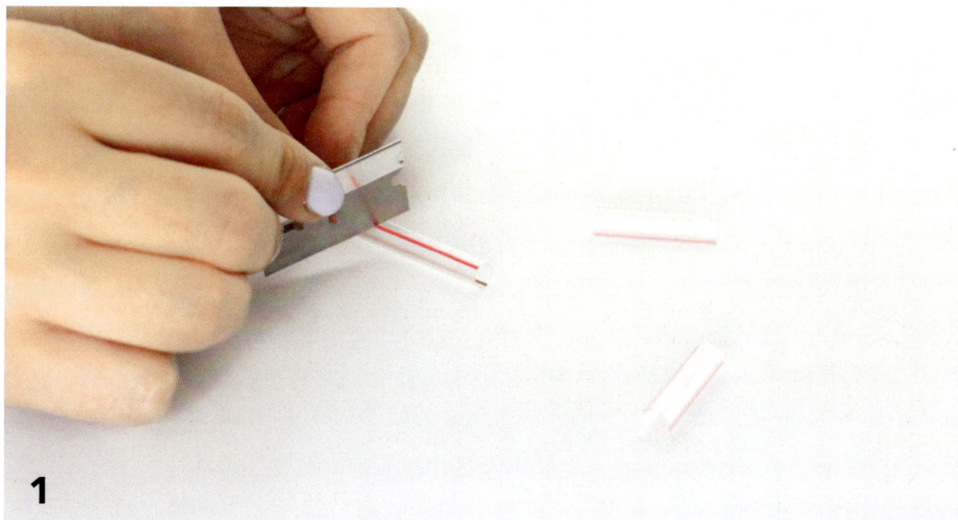

3. **Fill the straws.** Attach the clean-cut end of each straw to the tape so the straws stand up vertically. Fill the straws with sand, pebbles, and shells, leaving about ½" empty at the top. You could also use dry flowers, confetti, glitter, or colored resin. I layered my straws with sand, crushed turquoise, and a seashell on top.

4. **Add the resin.** Fill the straws with resin, leaving some empty space at the top for the screw eye pins. Work slowly, adding a few drops at a time so you don't overfill the straws.

5. **Finish.** Thread the screw eye pins onto a toothpick. Use the toothpick to position a screw eye pin over the opening of each straw. Make sure the ends of the eye pins reach the resin. You can also add the eye pins after the resin is set by drilling holes for them at the top of each pendant. Set the resin following the manufacturer's instructions. The UV resin I used required sunlight, so I placed my filled straws outside to cure for 30 minutes. After about 20 minutes, I placed the straws on their sides so the sun could reach and cure the resin at the bottom of the straws. Once the resin is completely cured, use a craft knife to remove the straws. Attach an earring wire to each screw eye pin.

3

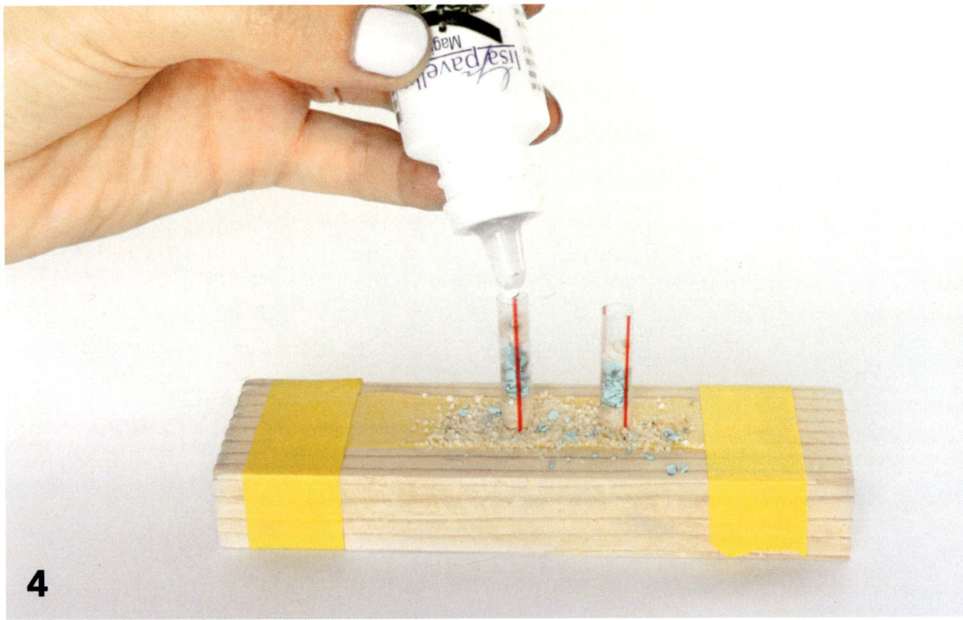

4

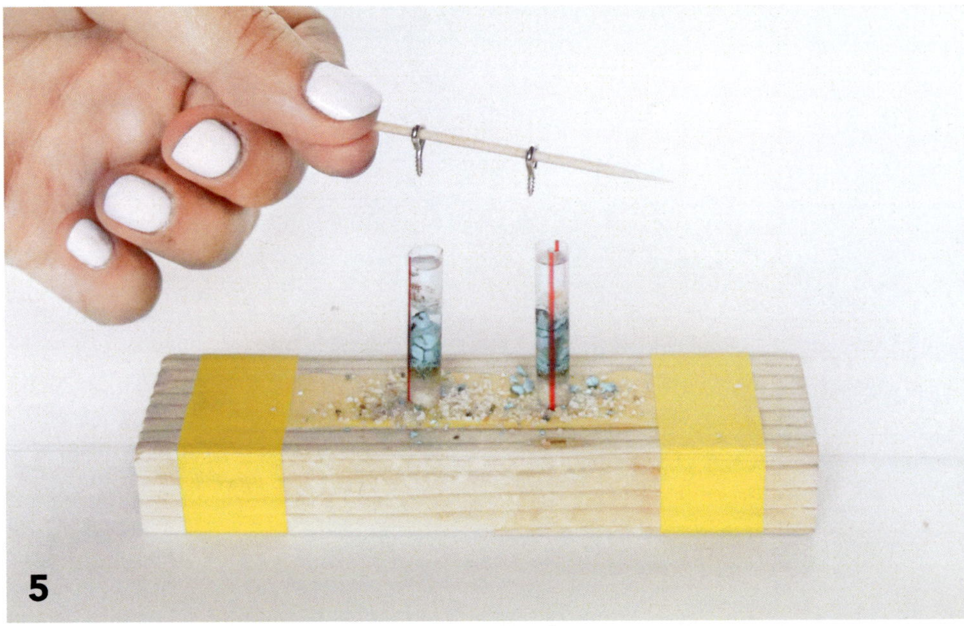

5

Seascape Keychain

Resin works best with silicone molds. The silicone gives the resin a smooth, glossy finish, and it's really easy to remove cured resin from a silicone mold. This beach-inspired keychain is a fun way to experiment with resin casting. The layering technique allows you to add different objects to the resin and control where the items appear in the finished piece.

Supplies

- Ice resin
- Silicone seashell mold
- Seashells
- Mini starfish
- Crushed turquoise
- Sand
- Keyrings
- Trigger snap hooks
- Measuring cup
- Mixing cups
- Craft stick
- Toothpick
- Drill

1. **Pour the first layer.** Mix the resin and fill your mold with a ¼" layer. Then, add the objects you want to be most visible in the finished piece. I added some seashells and a starfish. Let this layer set for at least 5 hours before pouring the next layer. The resin should be tacky, but solid enough that the objects you added to it won't move around. Use a toothpick to try to move the objects you added. If the items don't move around much, you're ready to pour the next layer.

1

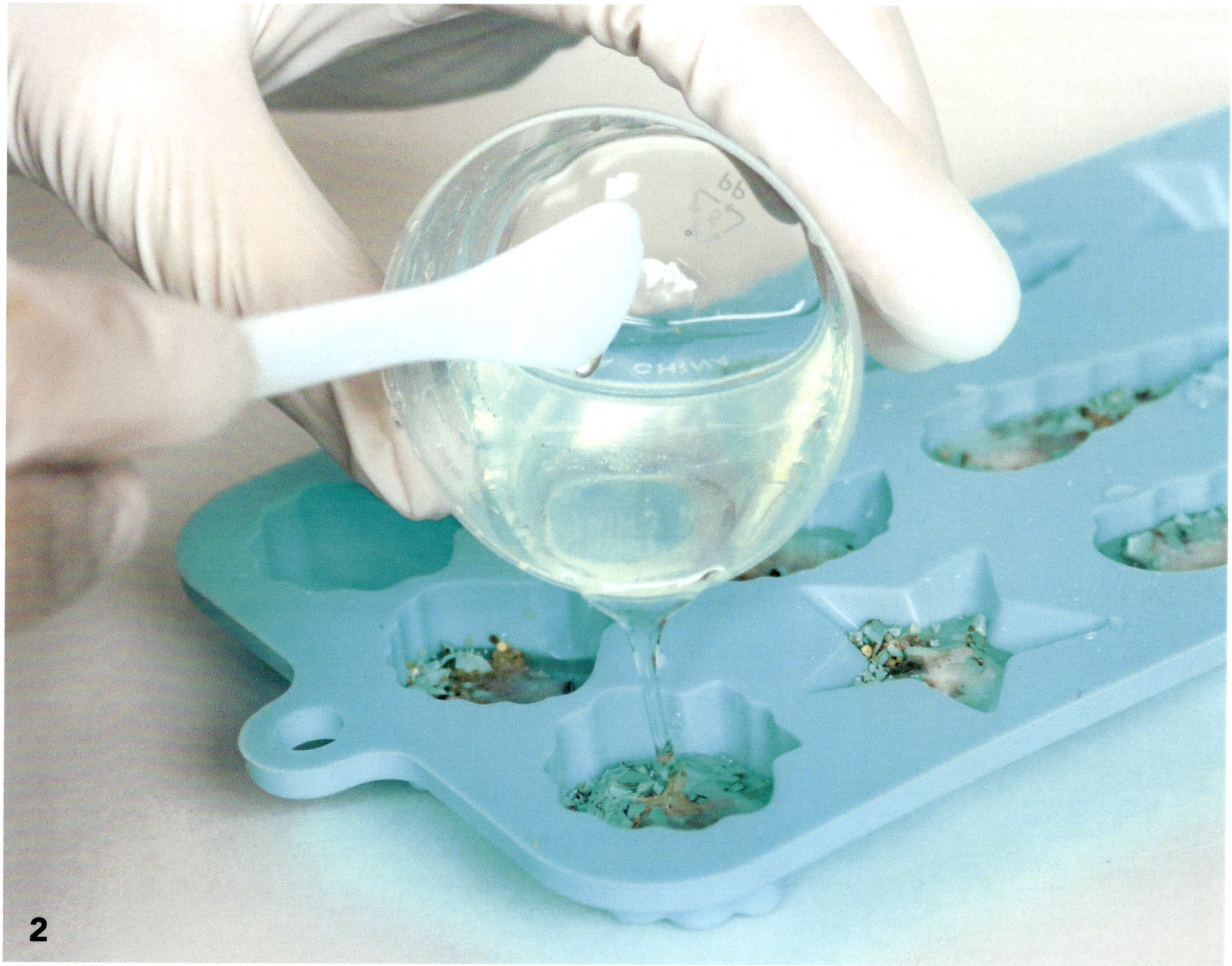

2

2. **Pour the second layer.** Mix more resin and pour it into the mold. You can make this layer as thick as you want depending on how thick you'd like the finished keychains to be. Add small objects like sand and pebbles to this layer. Make sure anything you add sinks into the resin completely. Allow the resin to cure for 24 hours. Then, drill holes in each piece for a keyring. Attach a keyring and snap hook to each one.

Preserved Flower Coasters

Can't stop falling in love with flowers? This project allows you to preserve your flowers so you can always enjoy them. Casting flowers is easy and creates some amazing art pieces. Preserving flowers from special occasions, whether they're from a wedding bouquet or a special anniversary gift, is a great way to hold on to those memories.

Supplies

- Casting resin
- Silica gel (I used Flower Drying Art® silica get from Activa®)
- Fresh flowers
- Silicone mold
- Container with lid
- Measuring cup
- Mixing cups
- Craft stick
- Respirator mask

Silica Gel

Silica gel is a sugar-like substance made to absorb moisture. Many artists use it to dry flowers because it's very gentle and has almost no effect on the flowers' color or form. Depending on the type of flowers you're drying, it can take anywhere from 2 days to 2 weeks for them to dry completely.

1. **Dry the flowers.** Drying your flowers correctly prevents them from decomposing in the resin. Consult the manufacturer's instructions for your silica gel and wear a face mask to avoid inhaling it. Pour a layer of silica gel into your container and lay the flowers on top, keeping the petals as neat as possible. I used flowers that were fairly flat so that my coasters would not be too thick. Cover the flowers completely with another layer of silica gel. Seal the container with a lid or plastic wrap and set it aside for 1 to 2 weeks.

1

Tip

If you're casting flowers that can't be flattened out, like a rose, experiment with different molds that better fit the flower's shape. For example, I've seen roses cast in a sphere.

2. **Pour the first layer.** Mix the resin and fill your mold with a ¼" layer. Gently place the dried flowers face down in the resin. Let the resin set for about 4 hours before pouring the next layer. If you can tilt the mold without the flowers moving, you're ready for the next layer.

3. **Pour the second layer.** Mix more resin and pour it into the mold. You can make this layer as thick as you want depending on how thick you'd like the finished coasters to be. Allow your coasters to cure for at least 24 hours before removing them from the mold.

Tip

Use flowers that have as little damage from drying as possible. Some flowers, like hydrangeas, are so delicate that resin will highlight any damage on them. Avoid checking your flowers multiple times during the drying process as this can damage the petals. Try not to remove the flowers from the silica gel until you're sure they're dry.

Photo Magnets

Photos are reminders of our favorite memories. Preserving photos in resin is a unique way to make these mementos even more special. Resin is perfect for preserving all kinds of memorabilia, like ticket stubs or a child's drawing.

Supplies

- Art or casting resin
- Mini photo prints (cut or sized to fit mold)
- Small square silicone mold
- Adhesive-backed magnets
- Measuring cup
- Mixing cups
- Craft stick
- Tweezers

1. **Pour the first layer.** Make sure your mold is clean and free of dust. Mix the resin and coat the bottom of the mold with a thin layer. I used a craft stick to help move the resin around in the mold, making sure I covered all the edges.

2. **Add the photos.** Use tweezers to gently place your photo prints face down in the mold.

BE
joyful

3. **Pour the second layer.** Mix more resin and gently pour it into the mold on top of the photos. I used a craft stick to help control the resin as I poured it. You don't have to wait for the first layer of resin to cure before pouring this layer. You can make this layer as thick as you want depending on how thick you'd like your finished magnets to be. Let the resin cure for 24 hours before removing the pieces from the mold. Attach an adhesive-backed magnet to each piece.

Library of Congress Control Number:2019952947

We have made every effort to ensure that these instructions are accurate and complete. We cannot, however, be responsible for human error, typographical mistakes, or variations in individual work.

Production Team: Technical Editor – Katie Weeber; Graphic Designer – Kate Moul; Photo Stylist– Lori Wenger; Photographer – Jason Masters

Made in U.S.A.